TECHNIC ETUDES

BY WILLIAM BAY

WBM09
ISBN 978-0-9859227-6-4

© 2012 BY WILLIAM BAY
ALL RIGHTS RESERVED. INTERNATIONAL COPYRIGHT SECURED. B.M.I.

Visit us on the Web at www.williambaymusic.com

PREFACE

The goal of these twenty etudes is to address various issues of guitar technique while presenting pieces which have melodic content, are interesting and fun to play and which can be used in concert or recital. Fragmented scale runs, scales ascending and descending several octaves, switching positions amidst musical phrases, arpeggio picking, string skipping and combining open and fingered strings are some of the issues addressed in these compositions.

It has been my desire to see the plectrum guitar utilized as a concert instrument in a manner similar to that of the classical guitar. My hope is that these studies may contribute to that goal. Other collections in this plectrum guitar series include **Short Etudes, Tangos, Preludes, Sonatas, Nocturnes, Psalms** and **Velocity Studies**. Additional plectrum guitar collections may be found on my website: **www.williambaymusic.com**.

Recordings are available for some of the books in the William Bay music catalog. These recordings may be found at **www.williambaymusic.com**. Please check my website for availability.

William Bay

CONTENTS

STUDY ONE IN D MINOR — 4

STUDY TWO IN E MAJOR — 7

STUDY THREE IN A MINOR — 10

STUDY FOUR IN A MAJOR — 12

STUDY FIVE IN D MAJOR — 15

STUDY SIX IN E MINOR — 18

STUDY SEVEN IN G MAJOR — 20

STUDY EIGHT IN C MINOR — 22

STUDY NINE IN A MINOR — 24

STUDY TEN IN E MINOR — 26

STUDY ELEVEN IN A MINOR — 30

STUDY TWELVE IN D MAJOR — 32

STUDY THIRTEEN IN C MAJOR — 34

STUDY FOURTEEN IN D MINOR — 36

STUDY FIFTEEN IN A MAJOR — 38

STUDY SIXTEEN IN B MINOR — 40

STUDY SEVENTEEN IN G MAJOR — 42

STUDY EIGHTEEN IN F# MINOR — 44

STUDY NINETEEN IN B MINOR — 46

STUDY TWENTY IN C MAJOR — 48

STUDY ONE
D Minor

Dropped D Tuning

William Bay

© 2012 by William Bay. All Rights Reserved. BMI.

STUDY TWO
E MAJOR

Moderato ♩ = 88

William Bay

9

STUDY THREE
A MINOR

William Bay

STUDY FOUR
A MAJOR

William Bay

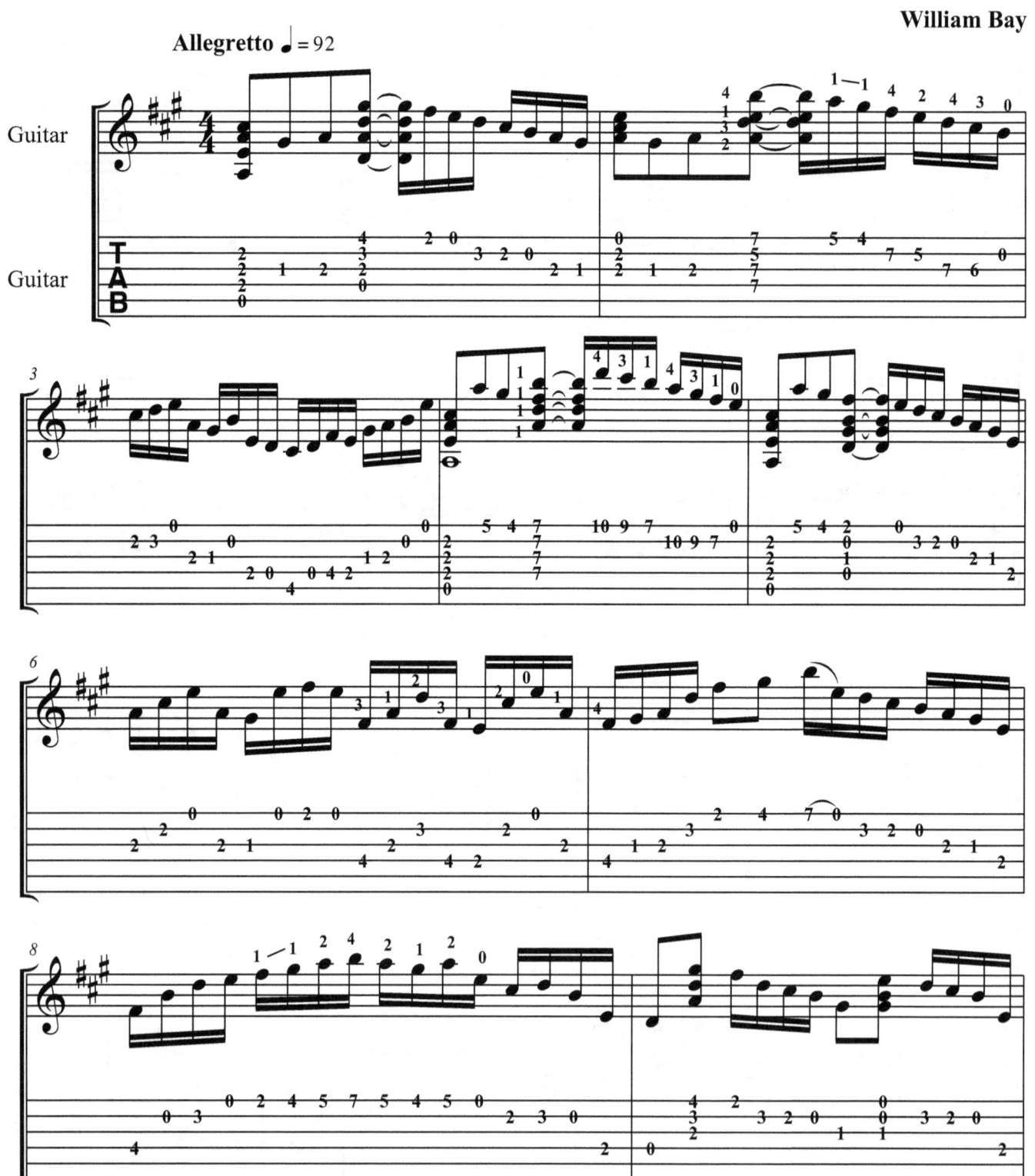

STUDY FIVE
D MAJOR

Dropped D Tuning

William Bay

Moderato ♩ = 86

STUDY SIX
E MINOR

William Bay

STUDY SEVEN
G MAJOR

William Bay

STUDY EIGHT
C MINOR

William Bay

STUDY NINE
A MINOR

William Bay

STUDY TEN
E MINOR

William Bay

This page has been left blank
to avoid awkward page turns.

STUDY ELEVEN
A MINOR

William Bay

© 2012 by William Bay. All Rights Reserved. BMI.

STUDY TWELVE
D MAJOR

Dropped D Tuning

William Bay

STUDY THIRTEEN
C MAJOR

William Bay

© 2012 by William Bay. All Rights Reserved. BMI.

STUDY FOURTEEN
D MINOR

STUDY FIFTEEN
A MAJOR

William Bay

STUDY SIXTEEN
B MINOR

William Bay

STUDY SEVENTEEN
G MAJOR

William Bay

Moderato ♩ = 80

STUDY EIGHTEEN
F# MINOR

William Bay

STUDY NINETEEN
B MINOR

William Bay

Presto ♩. = 104

47

STUDY TWENTY
C MAJOR

William Bay